Cursive Handwriting Workbook

Cursive Writing Practice Book for Kids and Teens

By Goldstar Workbooks

LEARN HOW TO WRITE IN CURSIVE!

CURSIVE IS A STYLE OF PENMANSHIP IN WHICH THE LETTERS ARE JOINED TOGETHER IN A FLOWING AND LOOPING MANNER FOR THE PURPOSE OF MAKING WRITING FASTER. ALTHOUGH MANY SCHOOLS IN THE UNITED STATES NO LONGER TEACH CURSIVE HANDRWRITING HISTORICAL DOCUMENTS SUCH AS THE UNITED STATES CONSTITUTION ARE WRITTEN IN CURSIVE AND DOCUMENTS STILL REQUIRE A SIGNATURE WHICH IS GENERALLY CONSIDERED TO BE WRITTEN IN CURSIVE. TEACH YOUR CHILD THE TIME TREASURED SKILL OF HOW TO READ AND WRITE CURSIVE THROUGH THE PRACTICE PAGES IN THIS BOOK.

WHAT'S INSIDE:

- LARGE 8 X 10 INCH PAGES AND A CURSIVE LETTER REFERENCE CHART

- TWO PAGES OF UPPER AND LOWER CASE PRACTICE PAGES FOR EACH LETTER

- SENTENCES TO PRACTICE CONNECTING CURSIVE LETTERS

- DOTTED LETTERS, NUMBERS, ARROWS AND A STARTING POINT DOT TO HELP GUIDE THE DIRECTION TO WRITE THE LETTERS

- BLANK LINES ON EACH PAGE TO PRACTICE WRITING ON YOUR OWN

- A LIST OF LINKS TO FREE ONLINE VIDEOS AND APPS TO HELP YOU LEARN HOW TO FORM CURSIVE LETTERS

Aa Bb Cc

Dd Ee Ff

Gg Hh Ii

Jj Kk Ll

Mm Nn Oo

P p Q q R r

S s T t U u

V v W w X x

Y y Z z

Upper and Lower Case Letter A

Upper and Lower Case Letter A

Connect the letters and write the sentences

Alina with an apple.

Alina with an apple.

Alina with an apple.

Upper and Lower Case Letter B

Upper and Lower Case Letter B

Connect the letters and write the sentences

Betty has a banana.

Betty has a banana.

Betty has a banana.

Upper and Lower Case Letter C

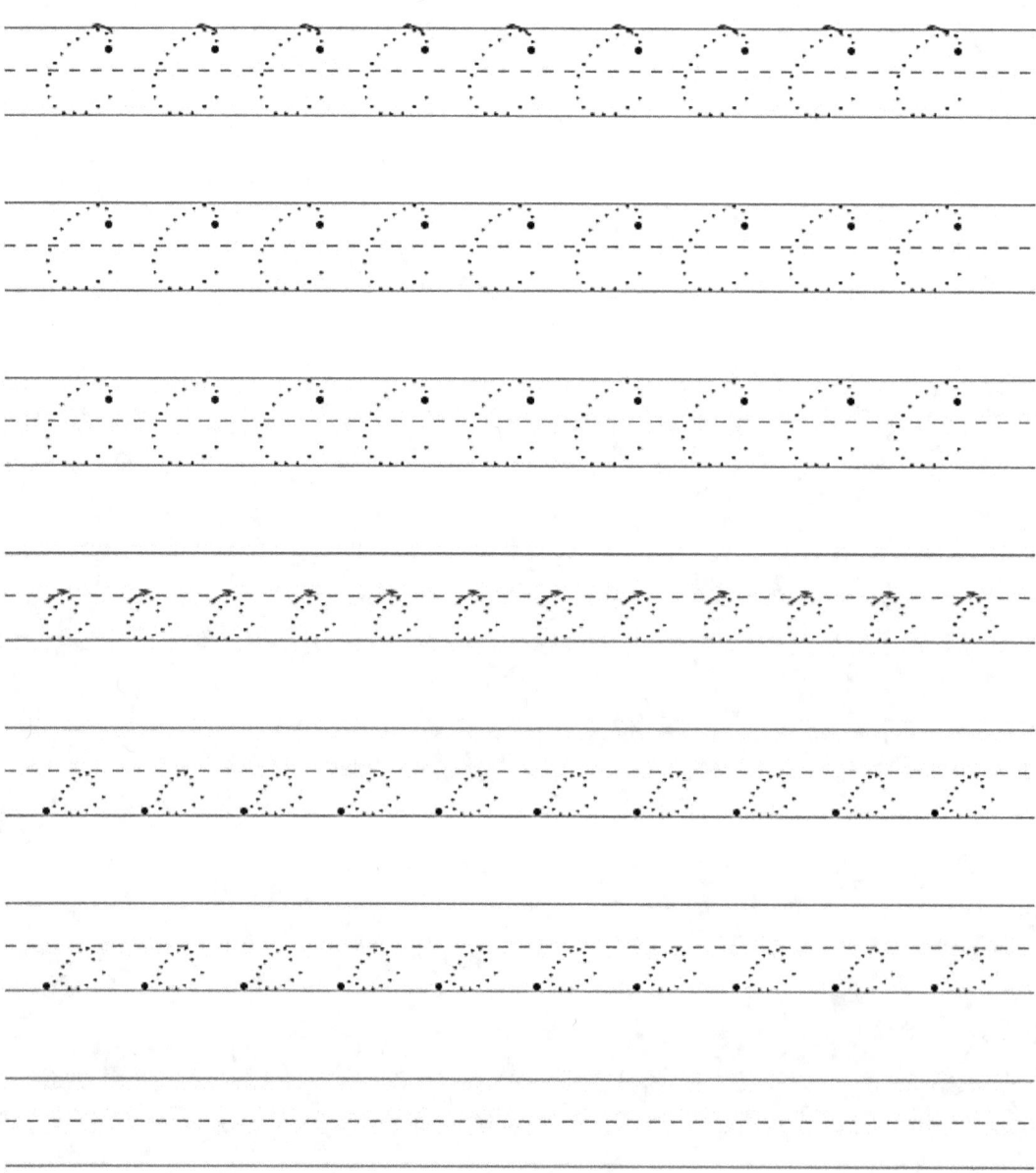

Upper and Lower Case Letter C

C C C C C C C C C

C C C C C C C C C

C C C C C C C C C

c c c c c c c c c c

c c c c c c c c c c

c c c c c c c c c c

Connect the letters and write the sentences

Cathy cuts a carrot.

Cathy cuts a carrot

Cathy cuts a carrot

Upper and Lower Case Letter D

Upper and Lower Case Letter D

Connect the letters and write the sentences

Danny dog eats dinner.

Danny dog eats

dinner.

Upper and Lower Case Letter E

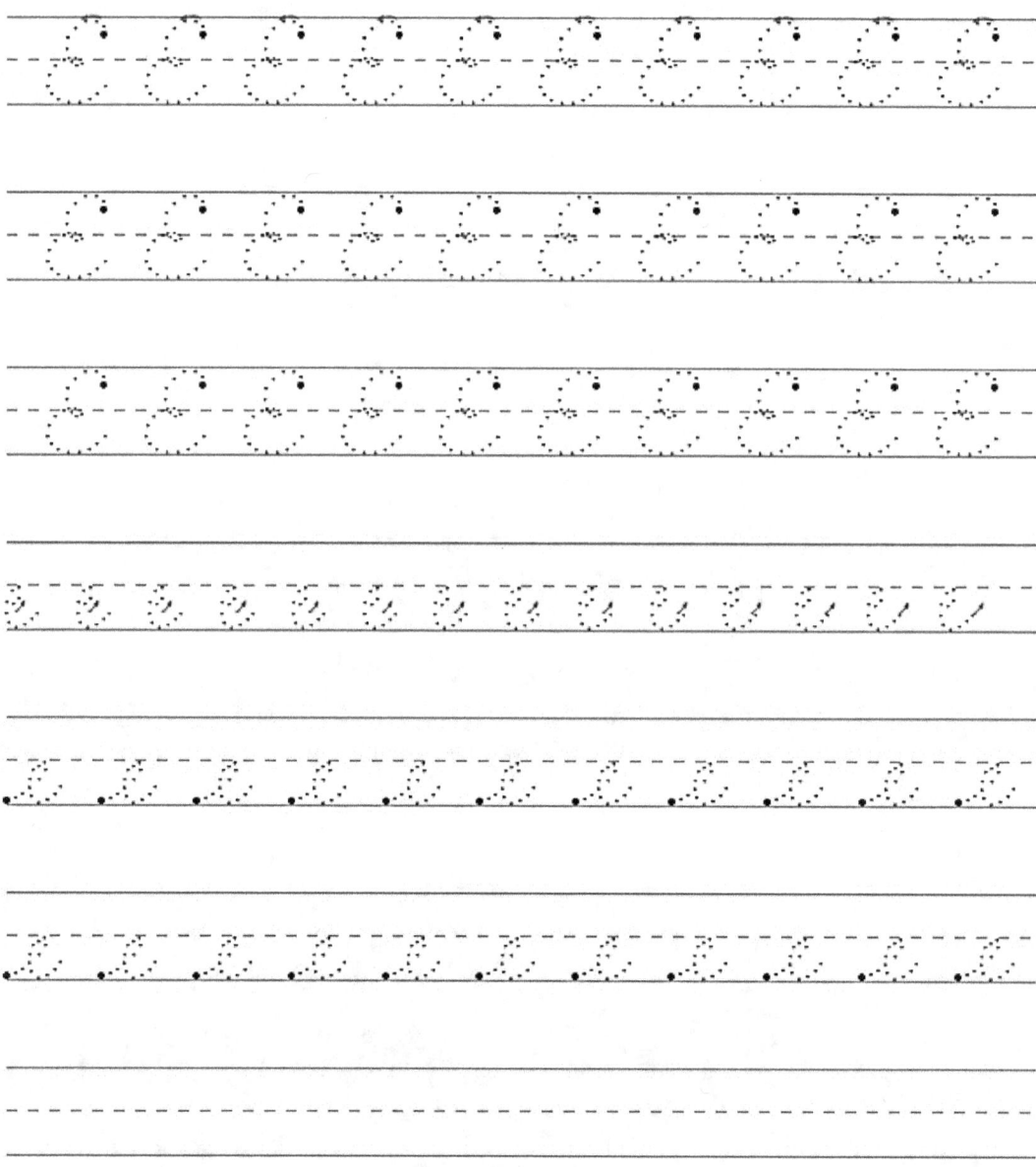

Upper and Lower Case Letter E

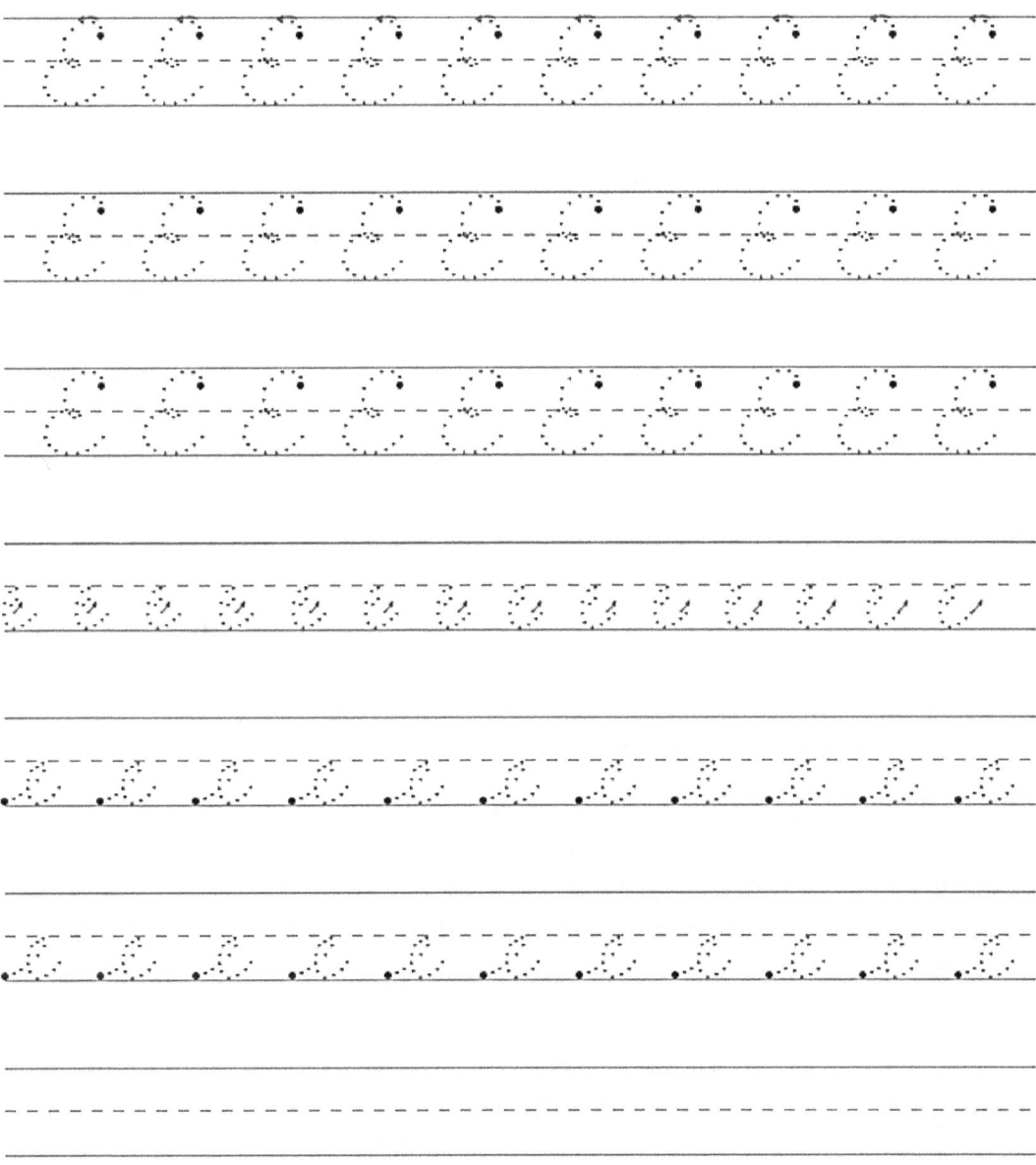

Connect the letters and write the sentences

(cursive handwriting practice — tracing lines)

Upper and Lower Case Letter F

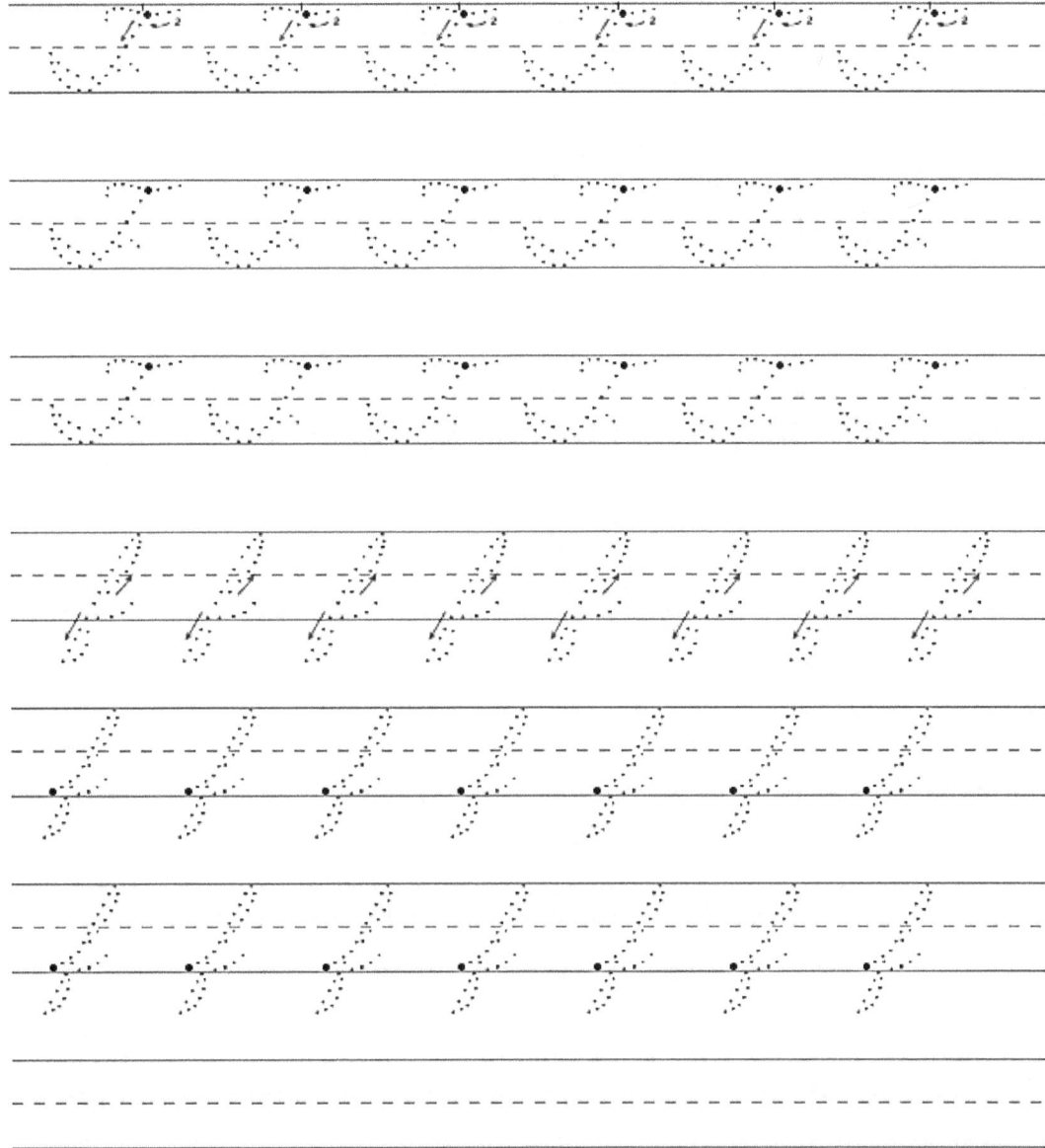

Upper and Lower Case Letter F

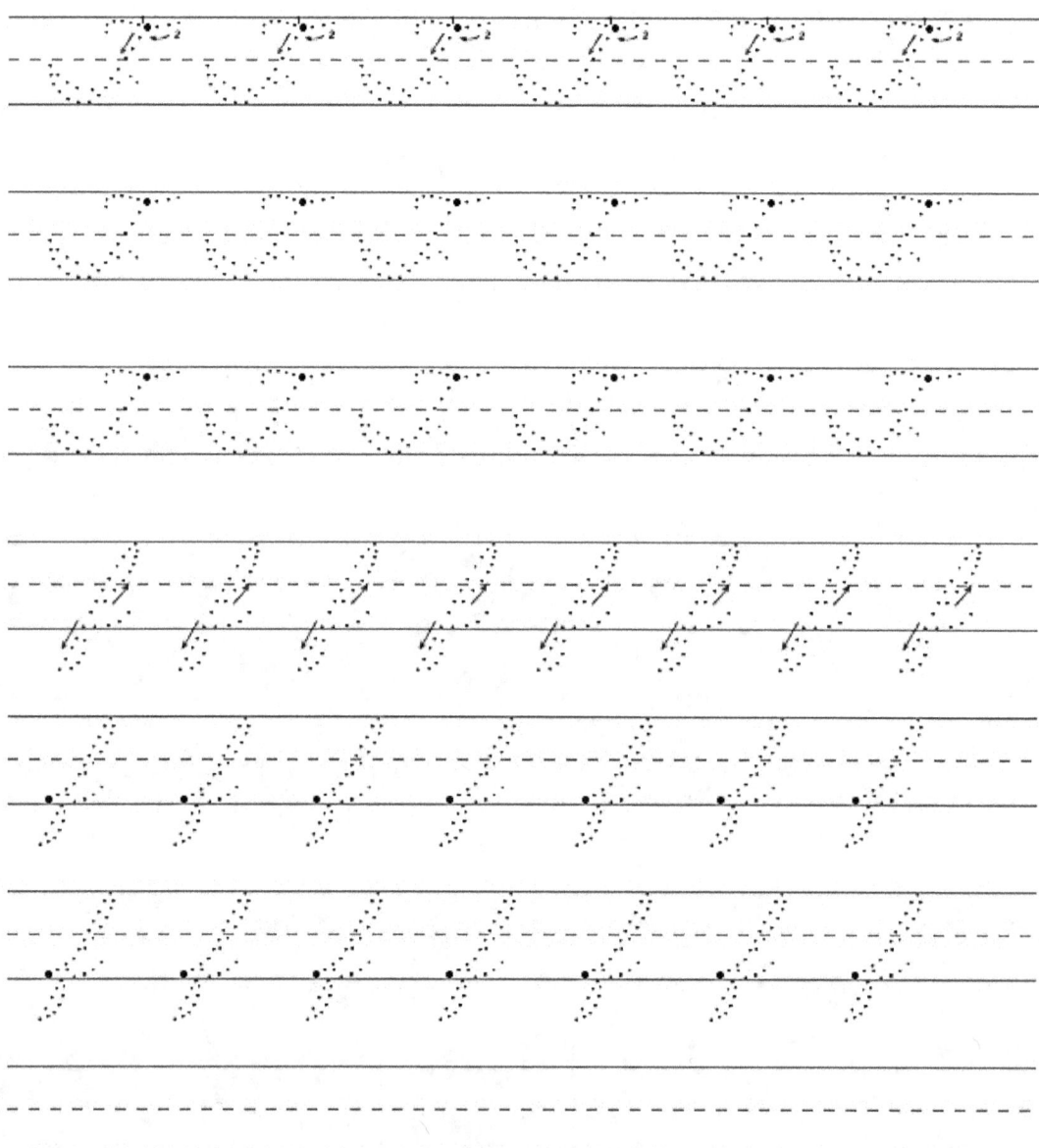

Connect the letters and write the sentences

Frank finds a farm.

Frank finds a farm.

Frank finds a farm.

Upper and Lower Case Letter G

Upper and Lower Case Letter G

Connect the letters and write the sentences

Bring you golfing.

Bring you golfing.

Bring you golfing.

Upper and Lower Case Letter H

Upper and Lower Case Letter H

Connect the letters and write the sentences

Writing has a holiday.

Writing has a holiday.

Writing has a holiday.

Upper and Lower Case Letter I

Upper and Lower Case Letter I

Connect the letters and write the sentences

Ida is in skating.

Ida is in skating.

Ida is in skating.

Upper and Lower Case Letter J

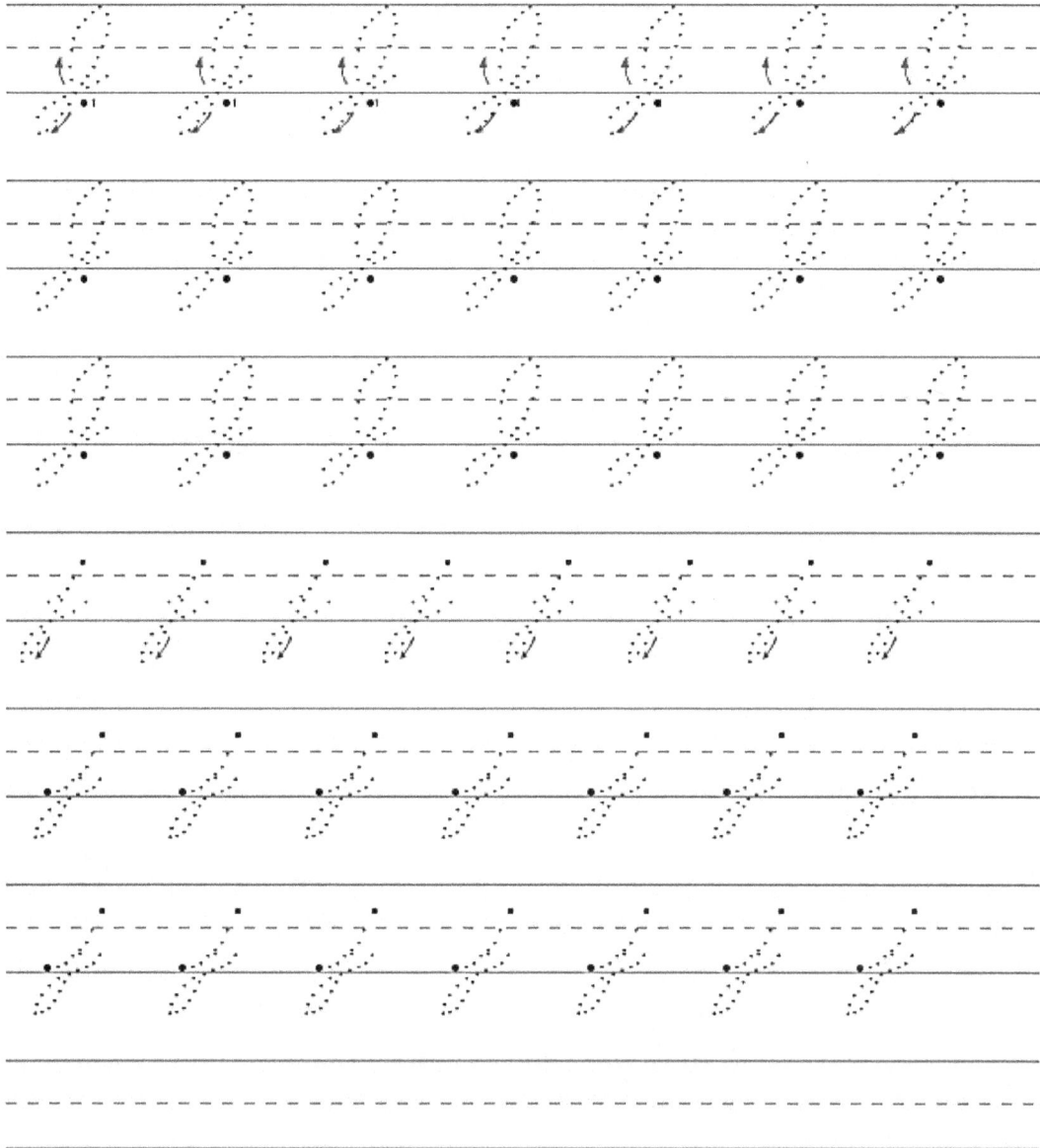

Upper and Lower Case Letter J

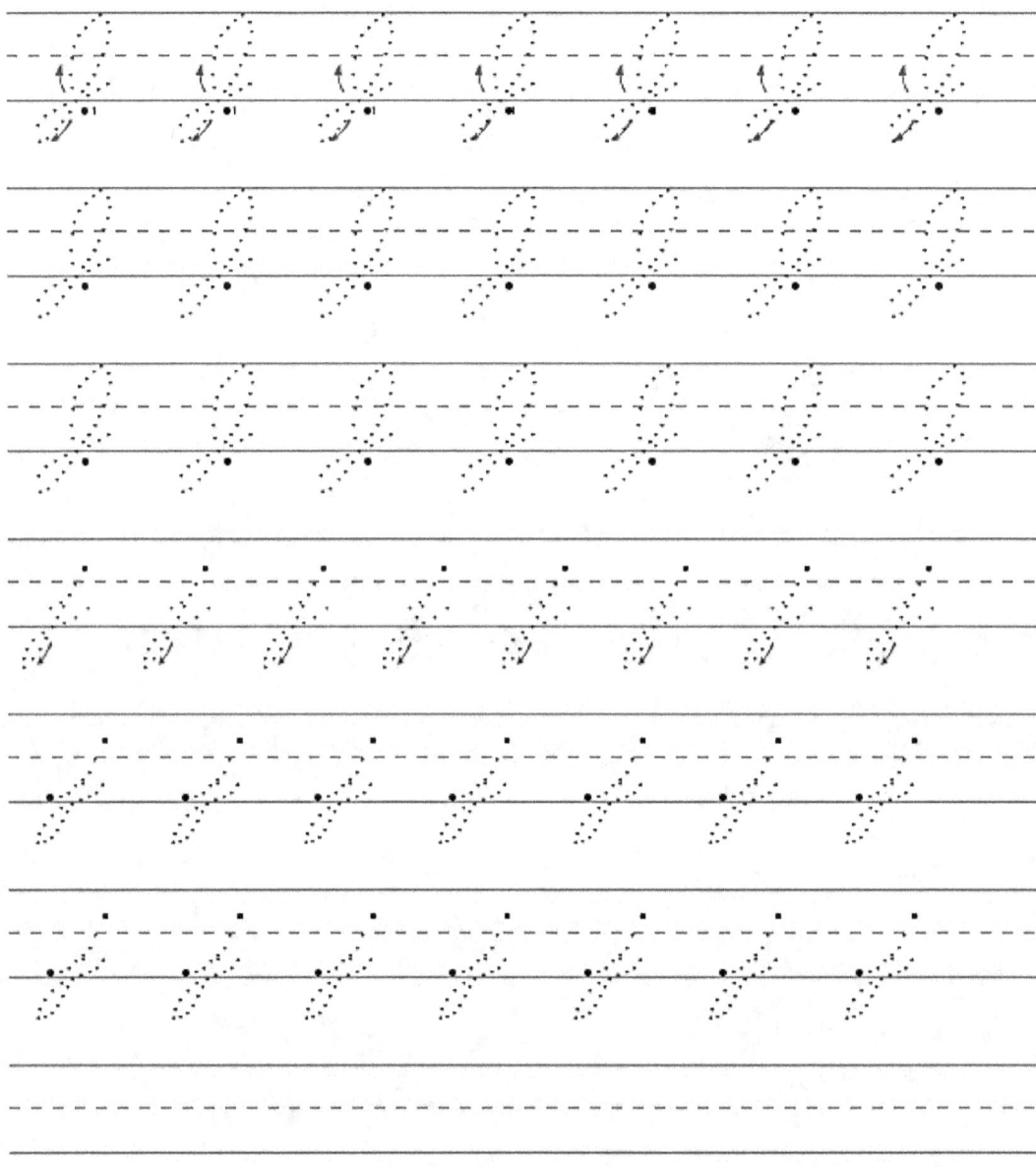

Connect the letters and write the sentences

Sandra jumps for joy.

Sandra jumps for joy.

Sandra jumps for joy.

Upper and Lower Case Letter K

Upper and Lower Case Letter K

Connect the letters and write the sentences

[handwriting practice — cursive tracing lines]

Upper and Lower Case Letter L

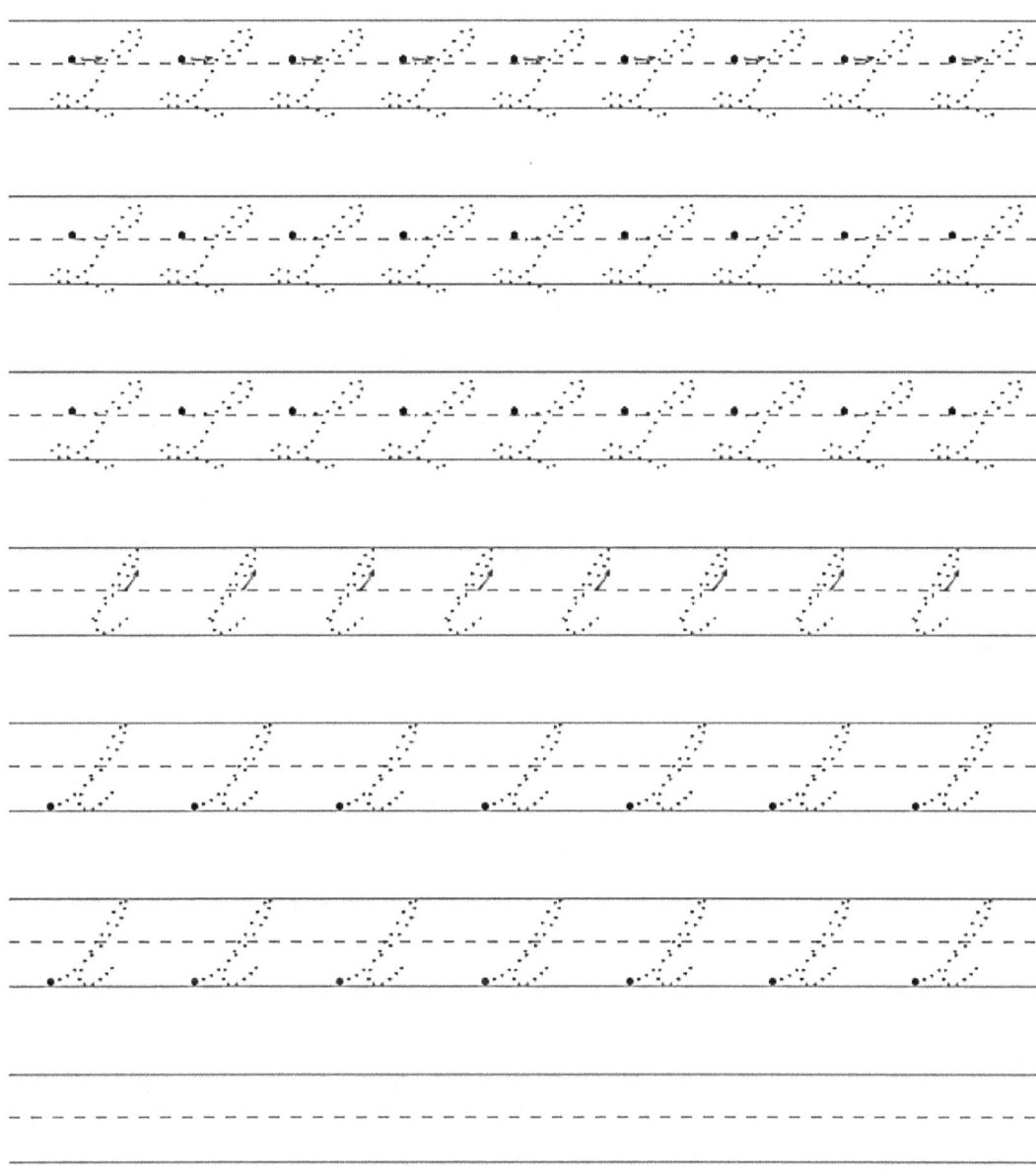

Upper and Lower Case Letter L

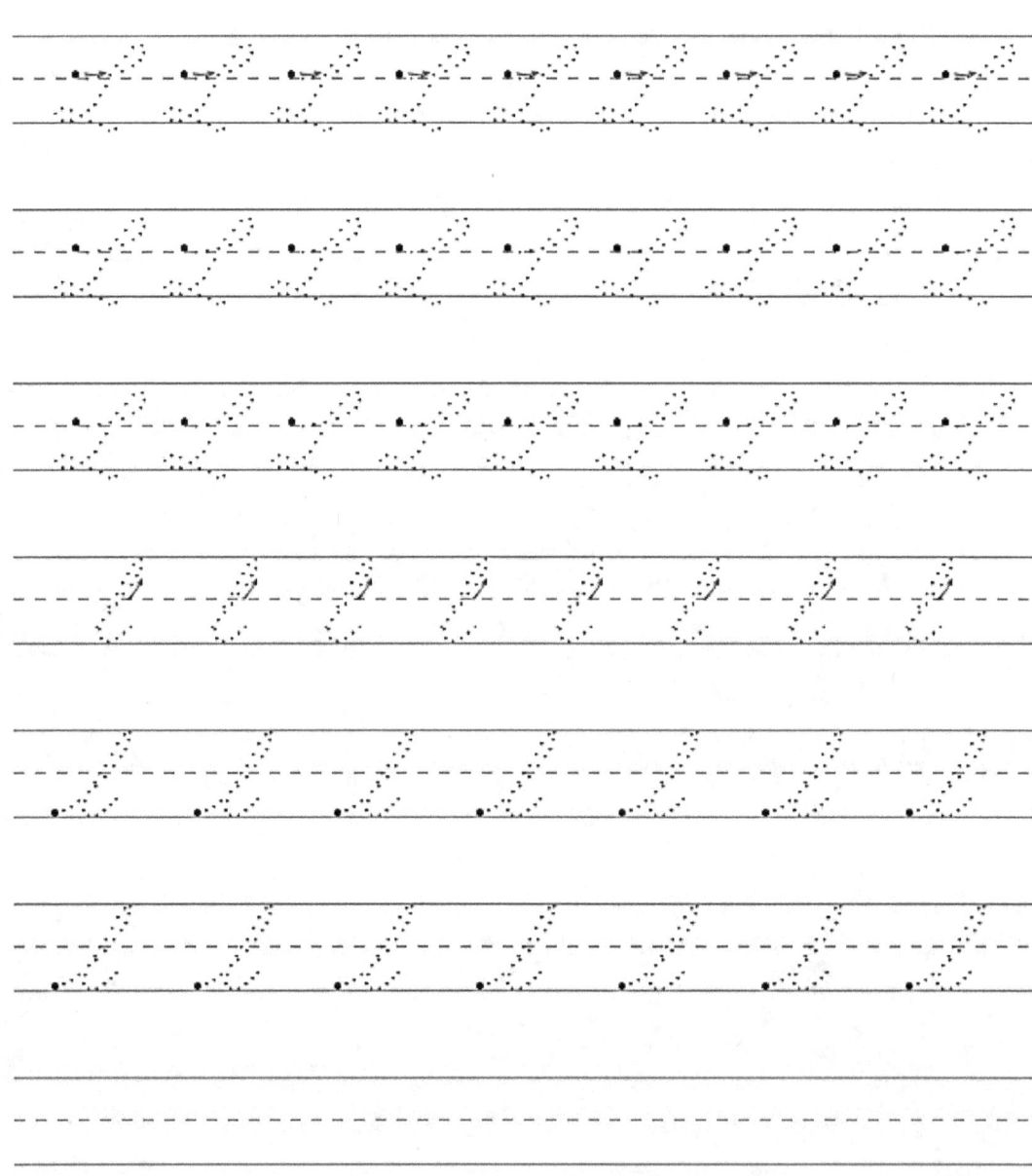

Connect the letters and write the sentences

Fanny loves John.

Fanny loves John.

Fanny loves John.

Upper and Lower Case Letter M

Upper and Lower Case Letter M

Connect the letters and write the sentences

Henry makes a map.

Henry makes a map.

Henry makes a map.

Upper and Lower Case Letter N

Upper and Lower Case Letter N

Connect the letters and write the sentences

Tima brang wanjara.

Tima brang wanjara

Tima brang wanjara

Upper and Lower Case Letter O

Upper and Lower Case Letter O

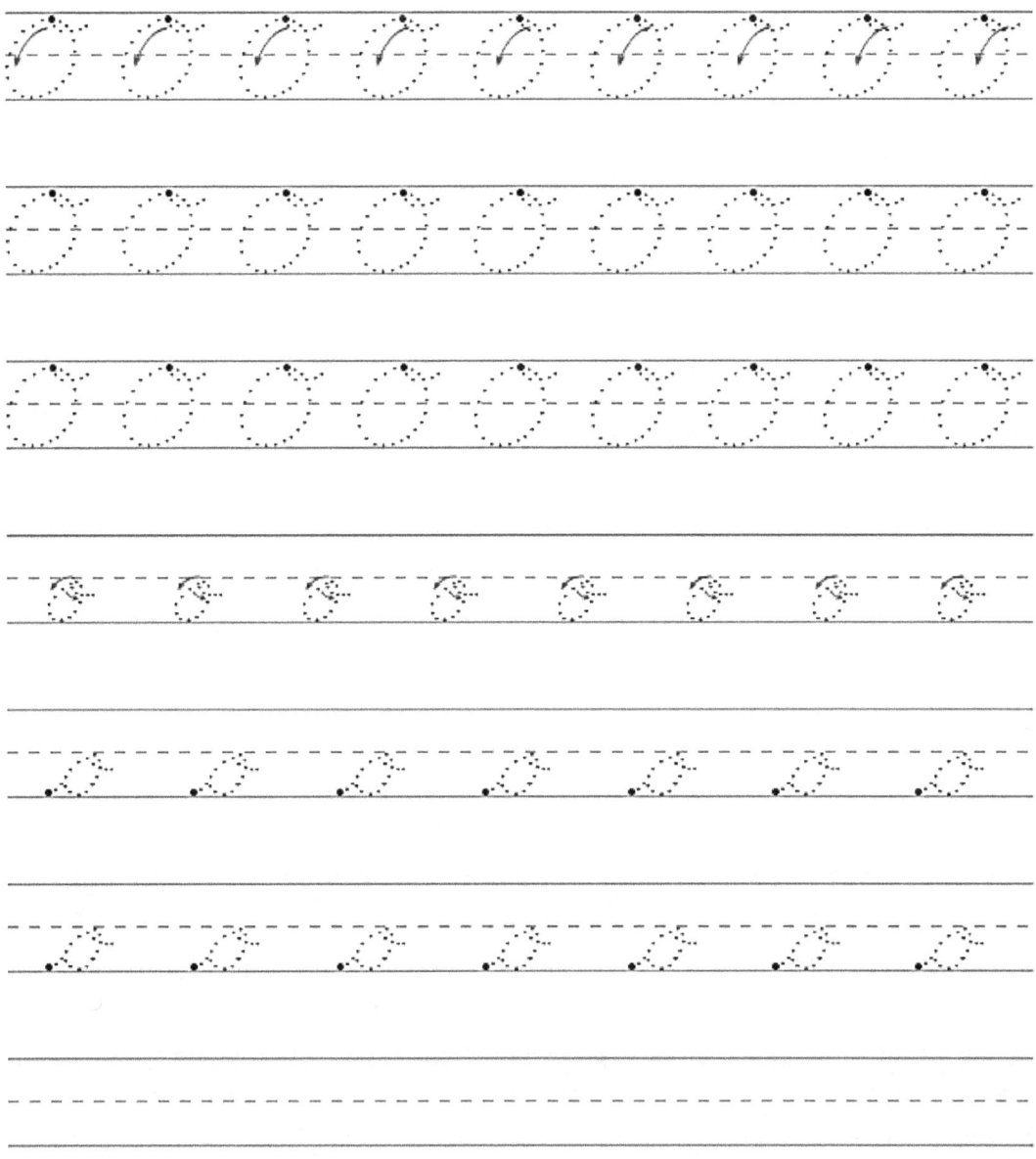

Connect the letters and write the sentences

She opened the door.

She opened the door

She opened the door

Upper and Lower Case Letter P

Upper and Lower Case Letter P

Connect the letters and write the sentences

Pets pity playful pigs

Pets pity playful pigs

Pets pity playful pigs

Upper and Lower Case Letter Q

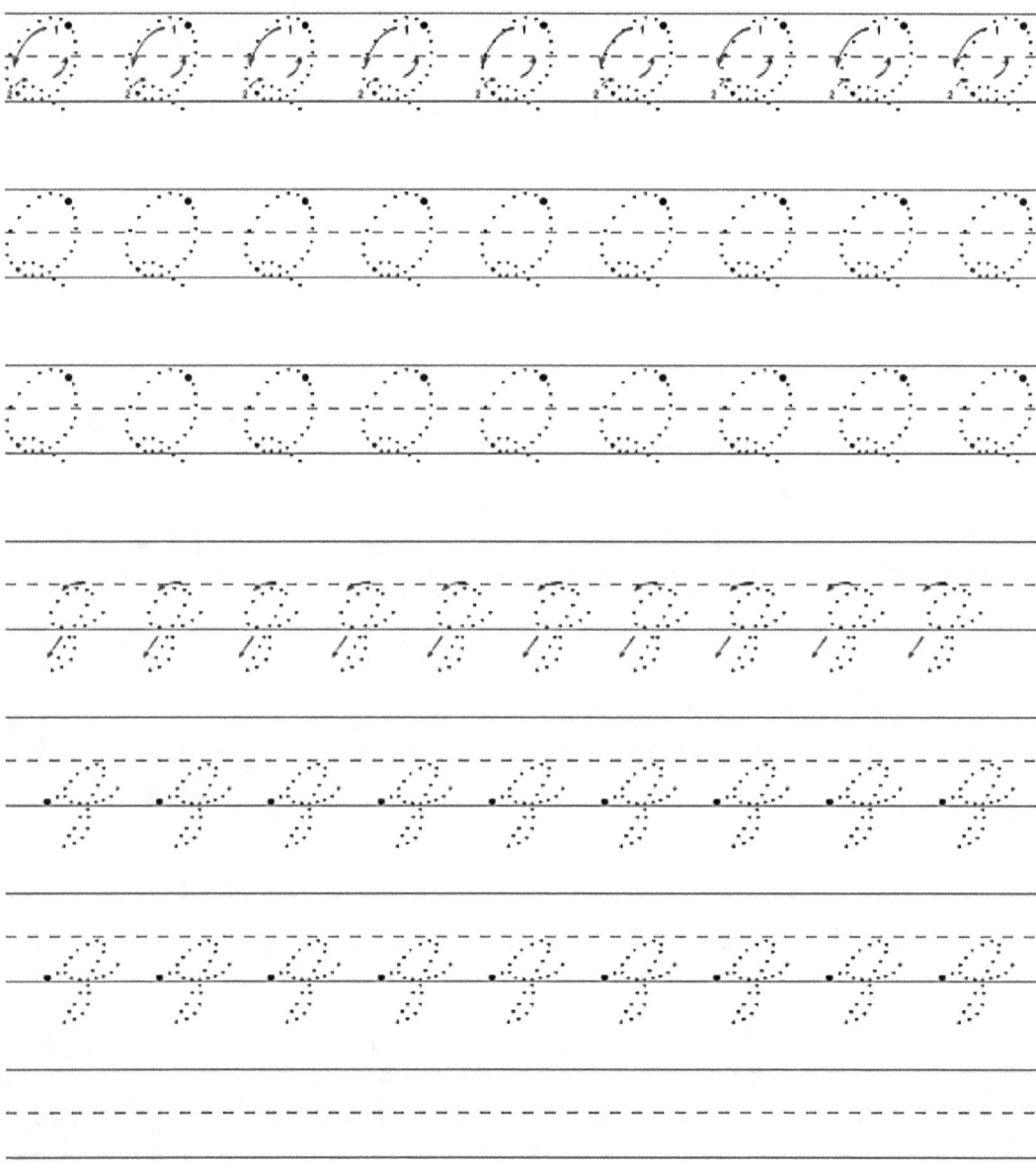

Upper and Lower Case Letter Q

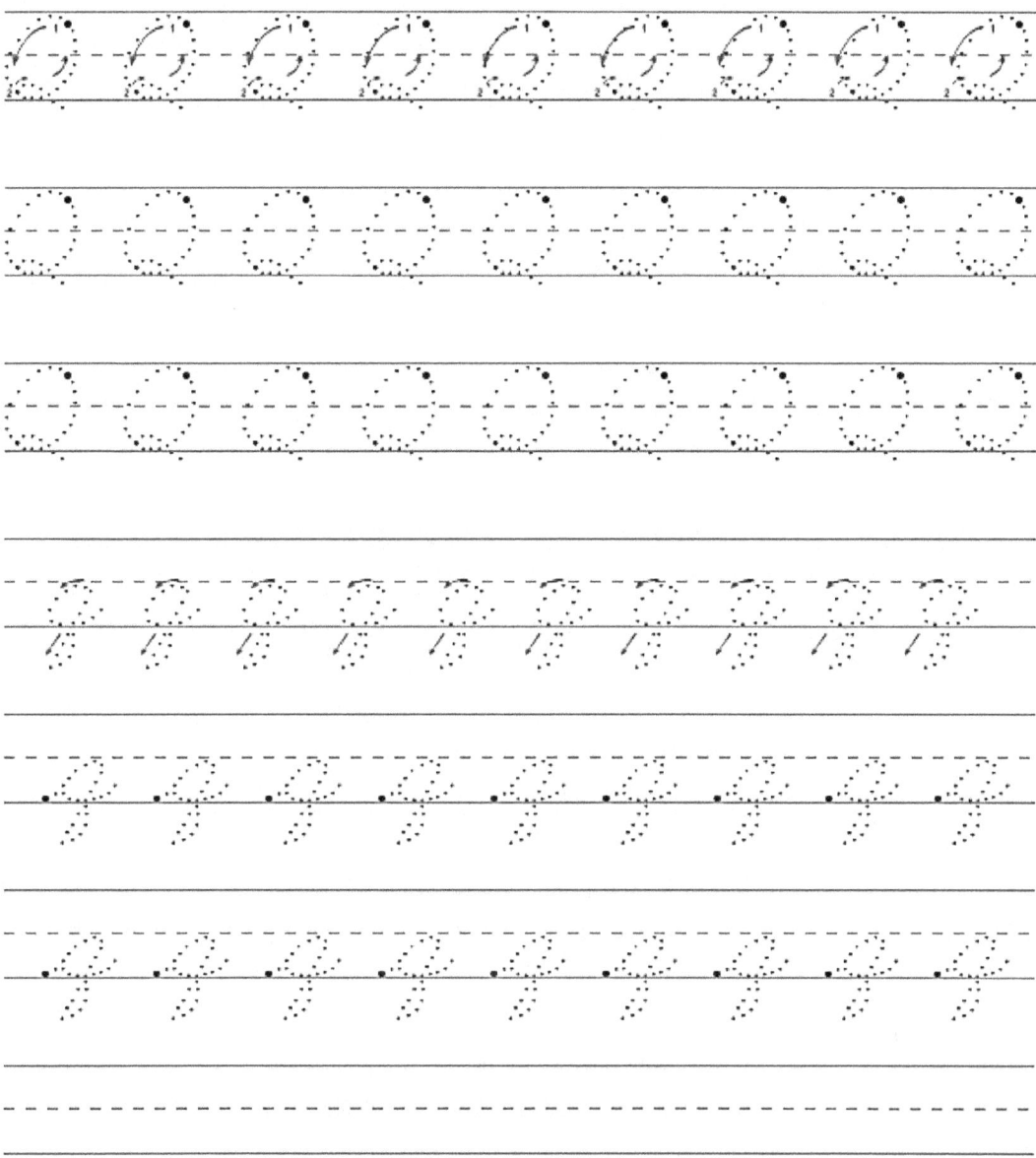

Connect the letters and write the sentences

Quinn put quidditch

Quinn put quidditch

Quinn put quidditch

Upper and Lower Case Letter R

Upper and Lower Case Letter R

Connect the letters and write the sentences

Aspen needs reports.

Aspen needs reports.

Aspen needs reports.

Upper and Lower Case Letter S

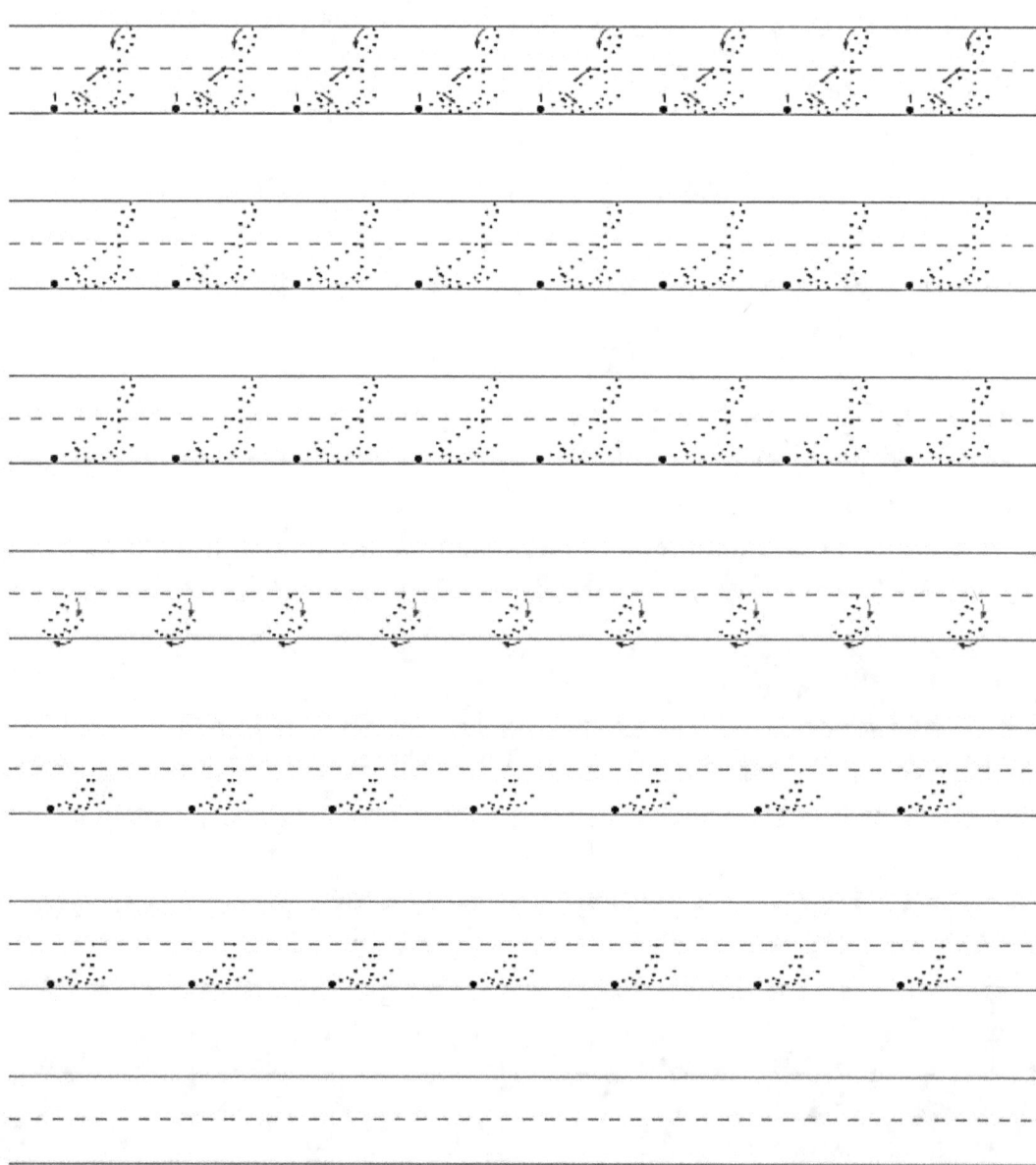

Upper and Lower Case Letter S

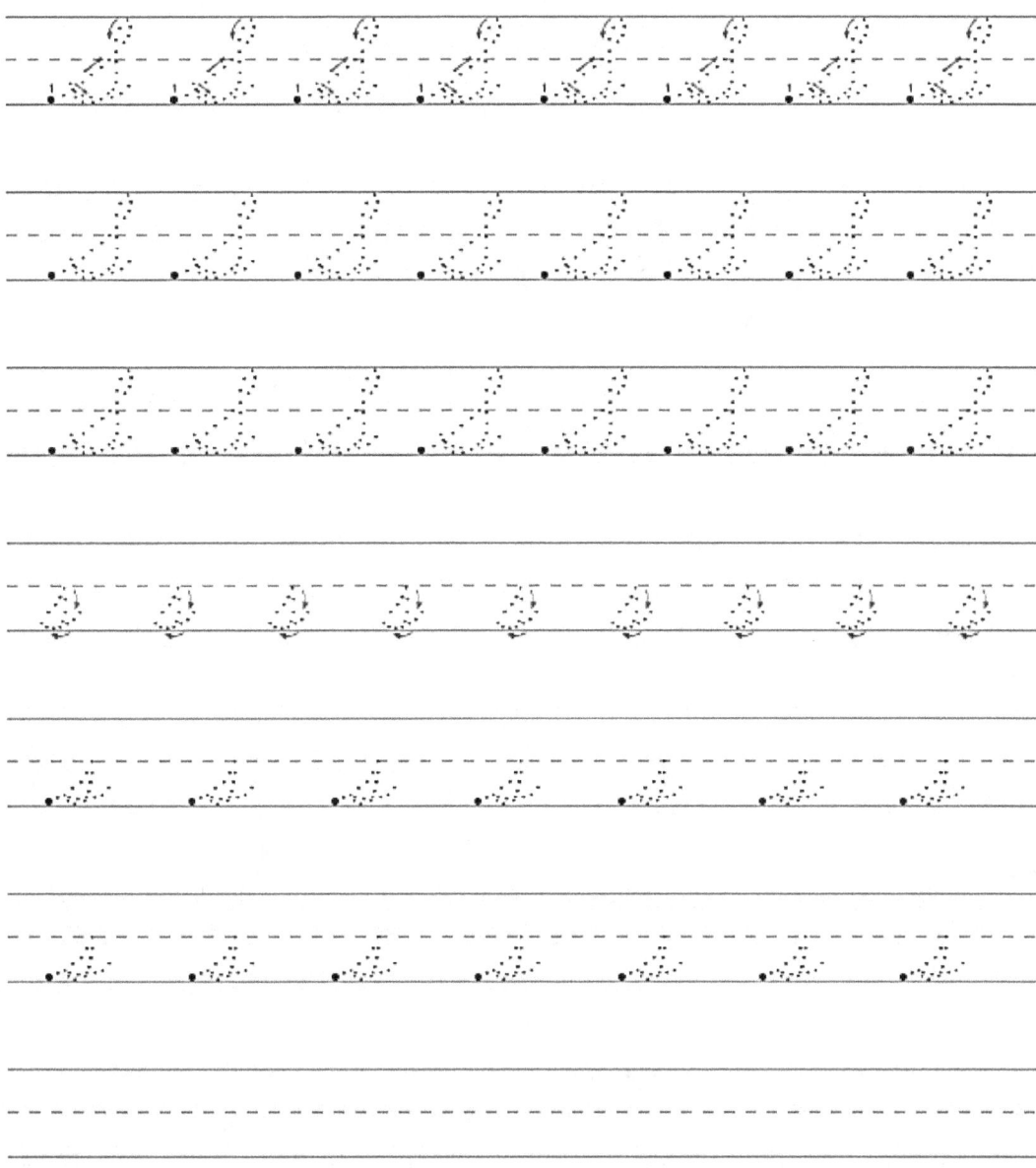

Connect the letters and write the sentences

Upper and Lower Case Letter T

Connect the letters and write the sentences

Tina Tabby a Tiger.

Tina tabs a tina.

Tina tabs a tina.

Upper and Lower Case Letter U

Upper and Lower Case Letter U

Connect the letters and write the sentences

Hippos were in

Australia.

Hippos was in

Australia.

Upper and Lower Case Letter V

Upper and Lower Case Letter V

Connect the letters and write the sentences

Water travels in a river.

Water travels in a river.

Upper and Lower Case Letter W

Upper and Lower Case Letter W

Connect the letters and write the sentences

Handler will walk to

meeting.

Hunter will ride a

zebra.

Upper and Lower Case Letter X

Upper and Lower Case Letter X

Connect the letters and write the sentences

Marion enjoying the xylophone.

Lauren enjoying a xylophone.

Upper and Lower Case Letter Y

Upper and Lower Case Letter Y

Connect the letters and write the sentences

Calendar always says

again.

Calendar always says

again.

Upper and Lower Case Letter Z

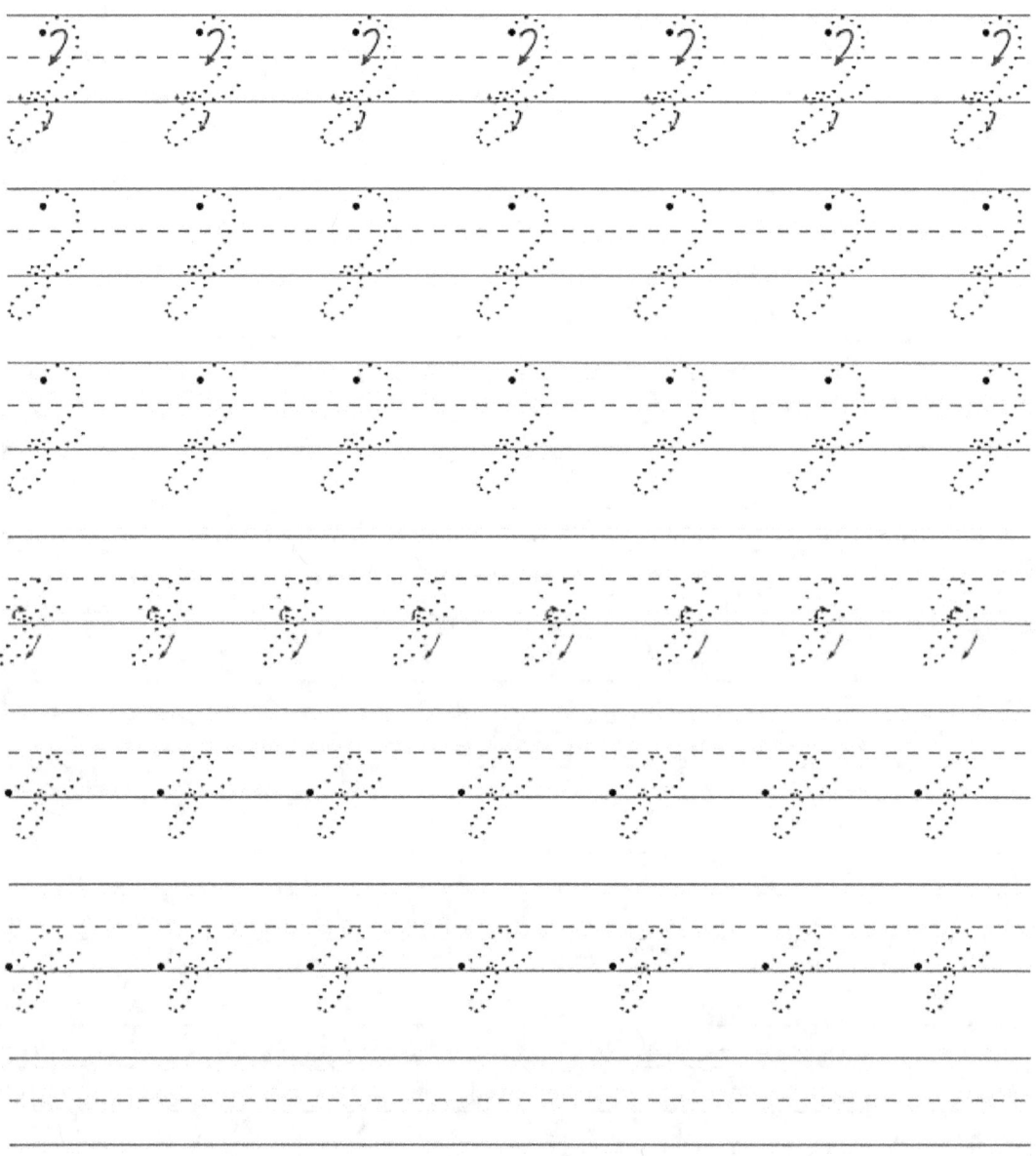

Upper and Lower Case Letter Z

Jack plays jing at

the zee.

Jack plays jump at

the zoo.

RESOURCES

**FREE ONLINE VIDEOS AND APPS
TO TEACH CURSIVE WRITING STROKE FORMATION**
*(PLEASE NOTE: ALL OF THE VIDEOS AND APPS LISTED BELOW ARE FREE
AND AVAILABLE AS OF THE DATE OF THIS PUBLICATION)*

YouTube Videos

Cursive Writing Wizard – All uppercase and Lowercase Letters and Numbers - ZB Style Font Cursive
By APPS for KIDS
http://bit.ly/2FV19Xu

How to Write in Cursive
By Sarzaya
http://bit.ly/2FVUZGz

Write Cursive Alphabets Uppercase and Lowercase Letters
By Super Smart Kids Club
http://bit.ly/2G5TjGk

Cursive Handwriting - How to Write the Alphabet - With Instructions
By Mister Teach
http://bit.ly/2ue7ms0

How to Write in Cursive Lessons 1-33
By The HEV project
http://bit.ly/2GbrC2t

Cursive Writing APPS

Amazon - Appstore for Android
Cursive Writing Wizard Trace Letters & Words
http://amzn.to/2pwOVKu

Crazy Cursive Lite
http://amzn.to/2IJHs2P

Write ABC - Cursive Alphabets
http://amzn.to/2px827h

Cursive Alphabets
http://amzn.to/2pwWOPV

Google Play store - Android Apps on Google Play
Cursive Writing Wizard
http://bit.ly/2ptMfNO

Cursive Writing
http://bit.ly/2pwlubf

Toddler ABC Cursive Writing
http://bit.ly/2pwWUqO

ABC Kids Cursive Writing
http://bit.ly/2uewQWp

Best Kids Cursive Writing ABC
http://bit.ly/2G1ec5E

Cursive Letters Alphabets
http://bit.ly/2u8vcW6

iTunes
Cursive Writing
https://apple.co/2IJLBnp

Crazy Cursive Letters Lite
https://apple.co/2pyp6ZL

LOOK FOR GOLDSTAR CURSIVE WRITING WORKBOOKS AVAILABLE ON AMAZON KINDLE AND PAPERBACK!

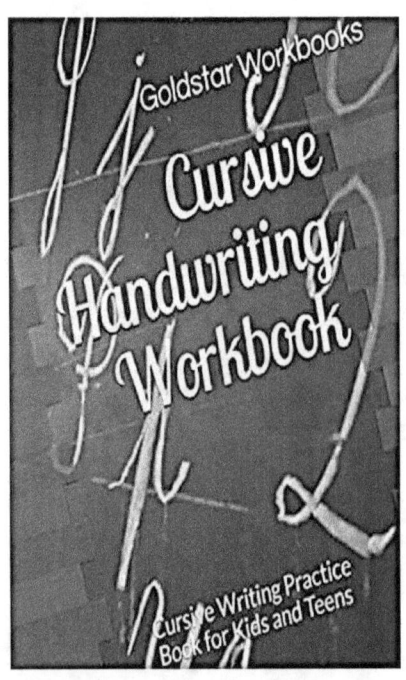

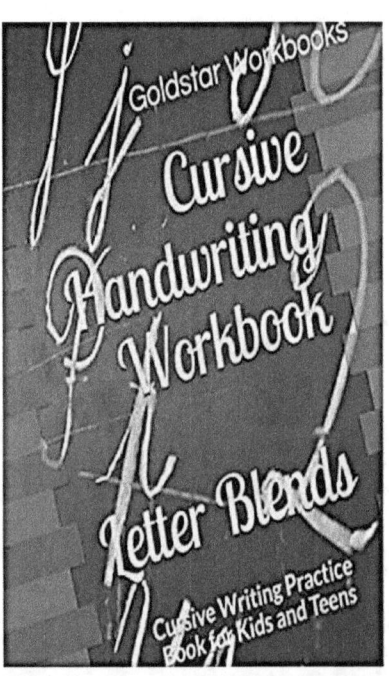

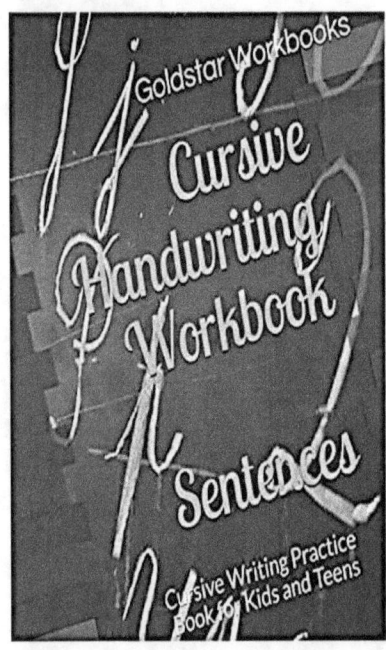

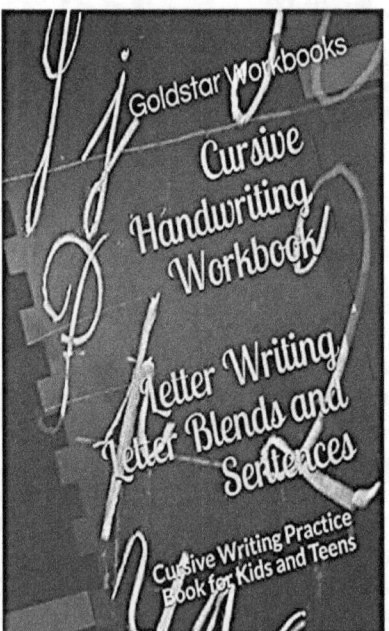

If you've found this book useful, please consider leaving a short review on Amazon

www.ingramcontent.com/pod-product-compliance
Lightning Source LLC
Chambersburg PA
CBHW060000230526
45472CB00008B/1876